Grayslake Area Public Library District
Grayslake, Illinois

THE MOST NOTORIOUS
CURSES
OF ALL TIME

THE LEGENDARY WORLD OF SPORTS

BY DAVE CAMPBELL

SportsZone
An Imprint of Abdo Publishing | abdopublishing.com

abdopublishing.com

Published by Abdo Publishing, a division of ABDO, PO Box 398166, Minneapolis, Minnesota 55439. Copyright © 2016 by Abdo Consulting Group, Inc. International copyrights reserved in all countries. No part of this book may be reproduced in any form without written permission from the publisher. SportsZone™ is a trademark and logo of Abdo Publishing.

Printed in the United States of America, North Mankato, Minnesota
082015
012016

THIS BOOK CONTAINS
RECYCLED MATERIALS

Cover Photo: Rusty Kennedy/AP Images
Interior Photos: Rusty Kennedy/AP Images, 1; AP Images, 4, 18, 23, 24; Anne Ryan/AP Images, 6; Morry Gash/AP Images, 9, 42; John Russell/AP Images, 10; Allen Frederickson/Reuters/Newscom, 12; Paul Sakuma/AP Images, 14; John Bazemore/AP Images, 16; Mary Altaffer/AP Images, 20; John Raoux/AP Images, 27; Al Messerschmidt/AP Images, 28; Phil Sandlin/AP Images, 30; Julie Jacobson/AP Images, 32; Mark Lennihan/AP Images, 34; Louis Lopez/Cal Sport Media/AP Images, 37; Kyodo/AP Images, 38; Kyodo/Newscom, 41; Dave Martin/AP Images, 44

Editor: Patrick Donnelly
Series Designer: Nikki Farinella

Library of Congress Control Number: 2015945547

Cataloging-in-Publication Data
Campbell, Dave.
 The most notorious curses of all time / Dave Campbell.
   p. cm. -- (The legendary world of sports)
 ISBN 978-1-62403-992-8 (lib. bdg.)
 Includes bibliographical references and index.
 1. Sports--Miscellanea--Juvenile literature. I. Title.
 796--dc23
                                                              2015945547

TABLE OF CONTENTS

CUB CRUELTY
CURSE OF THE BILLY GOAT

Is there really such a thing as a curse? How about a hex or a jinx? It all depends on your perspective. In sports, some teams just seem to keep losing big games in unusual ways. Their fans might think there is more at work than just bad luck. Others might believe the repeated letdowns are simply due to bad decisions and obvious mistakes. But one thing is certain. These so-called curses make good stories.

What better place to start than in Chicago? The Cubs are one of baseball's most beloved teams. Their roots on the city's north side trace back to the late 1800s. The Cubs still play in a brick-walled ballpark built in 1914. Going to a game at Wrigley Field is one

Sam Sianis—Billy's nephew—waves to the Wrigley Field crowd before a 1984 playoff game.

The Cubs tried to break the curse again in 2003 by inviting another goat to Wrigley Field.

of baseball's most charming experiences. But it was not so fun for a restaurant owner named Billy Sianis on October 6, 1945.

The Cubs were playing the Detroit Tigers in the World Series. Chicago won two of the first three games in Detroit. Sianis bought tickets to Game 4. One ticket was for him. The other was for his pet goat. Sianis thought the animal would bring good luck. However, its smell caused a big problem. Sianis was told the goat could not stay. He was angry. According to some accounts of the dispute, Sianis cursed the team. He declared that the Cubs would never win a World Series as long as his goat was not allowed in. The Cubs went on to lose the World Series in seven games.

Numerous attempts have been made to lift the curse. The team invited Sianis's nephew, Sam, to bring a goat to Wrigley Field for other playoff games. But through 2014 the Cubs had not been back to the World Series.

Facts are facts, of course, as a doubter might argue. The last time the Cubs won the World Series was 1908. That was 37 years before Billy Sianis and his goat showed up at Wrigley Field.

MOTOR CITY MADNESS

LAYNE HEXES LIONS

Since the Super Bowl began in the 1966 season, the Detroit Lions have been one of the biggest losers in the National Football League (NFL). There was a time, though, when the Lions were a dominant team. Their quarterback, Bobby Layne, was one of the grittiest players in the league. With Layne under center, the Lions won NFL championships in 1952, 1953, and 1957.

By the beginning of the 1958 season, though, Layne was splitting time at his position. On October 5 of that season, Layne had a rough game. The next day, the Lions traded him to the Pittsburgh Steelers for quarterback Earl Morrall and two draft picks.

The Lions' futility reached a new low when they went winless in 2008.

Layne was devastated. He was mad too. As the legend goes, Layne shouted that the Lions would not win for another 50 years. And he was right. Detroit has never even reached the Super Bowl, let alone won it. From 1958 through 2014, the Lions were 1–11 in playoff games. And in 2008, they became the first team to finish a regular season 0–16.

Lions fans have cause for hope, though. They might have found the perfect quarterback to end that curse. The season after the 50-year hex expired, Detroit drafted Matthew Stafford. Not only did Stafford and Layne both attend Highland Park High School in Dallas, Texas. They grew up on the same street.

AFTER THE MITCHELL REPORT
WHAT BASEBALL MUST DO

BY TOM VERDUCCI

Sports Illustrated

2007
Pictures
of the
Year

MAGAZINE MISHAPS
THE *SI* COVER JINX

Appearing on the cover of a magazine is usually a good thing. But some athletes hate being on the cover of *Sports Illustrated (SI)*. Athletes and teams have suffered a number of strange setbacks soon after appearing on the cover of one of the nation's premier sports publications. The magazine itself has acknowledged the jinx. It put a black cat on the cover of a 2002 issue. The headline read, "Is the *SI* jinx for real?" There is a mountain of evidence to support the possibility.

In October 2003, the Boston Red Sox and Chicago Cubs were in the baseball playoffs. Each team was one series away from the World Series. And *SI* put

Appearing on the cover of *Sports Illustrated* can be a mixed blessing—that is, if the *SI* jinx is real.

Superstar quarterback Brett Favre twice threw season-ending interceptions after appearing on the cover of *SI*.

Cubs pitcher Kerry Wood and Red Sox pitcher Pedro Martínez on the cover. Had they won, the two star-crossed teams would have met in the World Series. Instead, both the Cubs and the Red Sox blew leads. They not only lost their series. They added another chapter to each team's long and agonizing history of defeat.

In March 2006, *SI* put Duke's J. J. Redick and Gonzaga's Adam Morrison on the cover. They were two of the nation's top college basketball players. Duke and Gonzaga were both high seeds in the national championship tournament. Both teams lost on the same night in the Sweet 16 later that month.

Quarterback Brett Favre was on the cover right before his last two National Football Conference (NFC) championship game appearances. Both times—with the Green Bay Packers in January 2008 and with the Minnesota Vikings in January 2010—Favre threw a devastating interception late in the game. His teams lost both games and did not get to the Super Bowl.

Of course, there are just as many exceptions to the rule. After all, Michael Jordan is widely considered the best basketball player of all time. And he has been on the cover of *Sports Illustrated* 50 times.

4

VEXING VIDEO
MADDEN NFL
COVER CURSE

Each August, video game company EA Sports releases the latest version of *Madden NFL*. Many NFL players are among those eager to get their hands on a copy. And every year at least one player is featured on the cover of the game.

That might sound like a good thing, but some think otherwise. Players on the cover of *Madden NFL* tend to struggle in the next season. Some of the struggles make sense. The player picked for the cover is always coming off a strong season. It can be hard to match those totals the next season. But many of these cover boys go on to have bad luck on the field.

Troy Polamalu and Larry Fitzgerald might have had mixed feelings about appearing on the cover of *Madden NFL 10.*

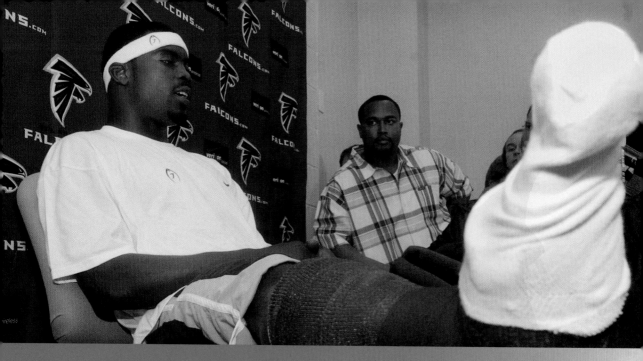

Falcons quarterback Michael Vick broke his leg shortly after appearing on the cover of *Madden NFL*.

Minnesota Vikings quarterback Daunte Culpepper tied for the NFL lead with 33 touchdown passes in 2000. He appeared on the *Madden* cover the following season. That year he threw almost as many interceptions as touchdown passes. And he missed the Vikings' last five games with a knee injury.

In 2002 Atlanta Falcons quarterback Michael Vick set plenty of records and made the Pro Bowl. He was picked for the *Madden* cover in 2003. Soon after the new version was released, Vick broke his leg.

Seattle Seahawks running back Shaun Alexander was the NFL's Most Valuable Player in 2005. He made the *Madden* cover the following year. Then he broke his foot. Two years later his career was over.

Of course the *Madden* curse does not claim a victim every year. Calvin Johnson's spectacular 2012 season is the best evidence of that. The Detroit Lions wide receiver set an NFL single-season record with 1,964 receiving yards after appearing on the cover.

COACH BUYS INTO CURSE

In time the cover subject came to be determined by public vote. In 2014 the two finalists were Carolina Panthers quarterback Cam Newton and Seattle Seahawks cornerback Richard Sherman. That summer Newton's coach, Ron Rivera, was asked which player he would pick. He said he would go with Sherman. Why? "I'm trying to avoid the jinx," Rivera said with a smile.

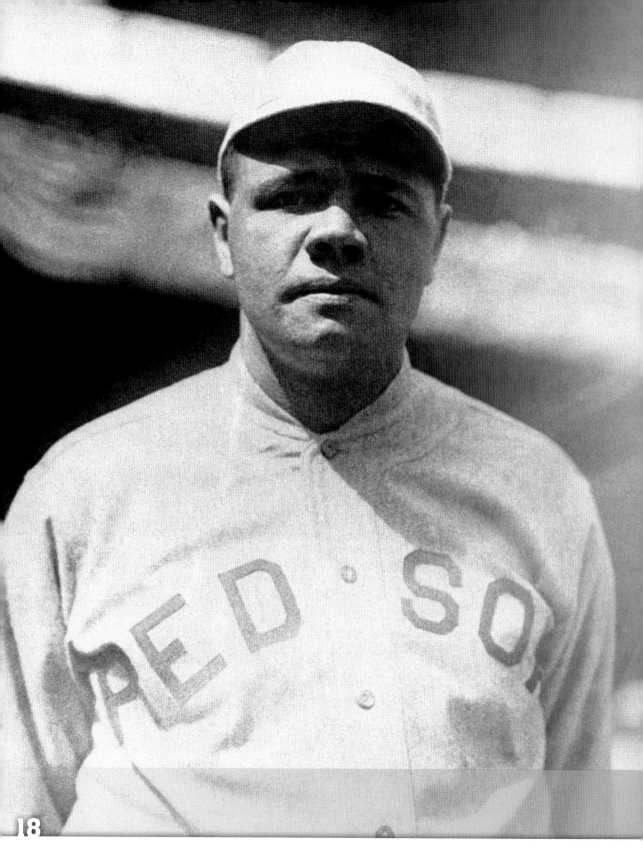

5

RED SOX BLUES
CURSE OF THE BAMBINO

Boston Red Sox fans finally found out that curses can be broken. They just had to be patient for 86 years.

Trouble began when the Red Sox sold Babe Ruth to the New York Yankees. Ruth was a larger-than-life player who was also called "the Bambino." He started playing for Boston in 1914. Ruth was a pitcher at first, and a very good one. He helped Boston win three World Series between 1915 and 1918. But cash was tight for owner Harry Frazee. So before the 1920 season, he did the unthinkable. He sent Ruth to the Yankees for $100,000.

Babe Ruth was a star pitcher and outfielder for the Red Sox before he was sold to the Yankees.

Red Sox fans decorated the grave of Babe Ruth after their beloved team finally broke the Curse of the Bambino in 2004.

Ruth, of course, went on to become one of baseball's greatest sluggers. And the Curse of the Bambino was born. Ruth hit 54 home runs in 1920. That was more than any American League *team* hit that year. He finished his career with 714 homers. That stood as the Major League Baseball record for nearly

40 years. The Yankees won their first four World Series with Ruth on the team.

Meanwhile the Red Sox suffered through a history filled with missed chances. The lowest point came in 1986. They were one strike away from finally winning the World Series. But the New York Mets rallied to tie Game 6. Then first baseman Bill Buckner let a ball go between his legs to give the Mets the winning run in Game 6. They beat the Red Sox again in Game 7.

The Red Sox finally won the World Series in 2004. That was 86 years after they had sold Ruth. The Yankees won 26 titles in that stretch. Boston won it again in 2007 and 2013. The Curse of the Bambino was finally over.

6

SOCCER SHENANIGANS
WITCH DOCTOR

Stories of curses can be found overseas too. Take Australia's men's national soccer team. The team known as the Socceroos had an important match in Africa in 1969. They hired a witch doctor to hex their opponent. It worked—or at least the Socceroos won. But the witch doctor did not get paid, so he reversed the curse. Australia lost its next match to Israel when three players fell ill.

In 1974 the Socceroos reached the World Cup for the first time. But they were eliminated in the group stage without scoring a single goal. Tough losses piled up, such as in 1997 when they blew a 2-0 lead against Iran. The teams played to a draw. With a win Australia would have qualified for the World Cup.

The Socceroos did not score a goal at the 1974 World Cup. Was a witch doctor's curse to blame?

But the mystery deepened. Johnny Warren, one of Australia's greatest players, wrote a book about his career. In it, he revealed the witch doctor story. Fellow Australian John Safran, a comedian and filmmaker, read Warren's book. In 2004 Safran tried to end the curse. He hired another witch doctor in an attempt to reverse the spell.

And again, it worked—or at least the Socceroos' fortunes changed for the better. They qualified for the next three World Cups. And in 2006 they advanced past the group stage for the first time.

7

ANDRETTIS' AGONY
IMPASSE AT INDY

The Andretti family is one of the most famous in the history of auto racing. Their daring driving has spanned three generations. Five Andrettis have raced professionally. But they are in the midst of a 40-plus-year dry spell in the sport's biggest race.

Mario Andretti won the Indianapolis 500 in 1969. None of the Andrettis have taken first place in the so-called Greatest Spectacle in Racing since. Not Mario. Not sons Michael or Jeff. Not nephew John. Not grandson Marco, whose sixth-place finish in 2015 was the seventieth time an Andretti sat behind the wheel at the Indy 500.

Mario Andretti waves to his fans after winning the 1969 Indianapolis 500.

The Andretti Curse can be traced back to Mario's victory in 1969. Since then it has been nothing but heartache at the Brickyard for the family.

In 1981 Mario finished second to Bobby Unser. He held the title briefly when Unser was penalized for passing cars illegally. Months later an appeal of that decision returned victory to Unser. In 1992 both Mario and Jeff were badly injured in a crash. Marco lost in 2006 by a fraction of a second. Sam Hornish Jr. passed him just feet before the finish line. Michael was third. And Michael holds the Indy 500 career record for most laps led (431) without winning.

The Andrettis have not denied that pressure to win at Indy has built over the years.

"We just have to keep the frustration from sitting in too much and just realize that we have a good shot at it every year," Marco said.

Sam Hornish Jr., *right*, slips past Marco Andretti at the finish line of the 2006 Indianapolis 500.

8

CHEER CONTROVERSY
BAD NEWS, BEARS

Chicago's least favorite animal has to be the billy goat. But for those who believe in curses, the Honey Bears are probably a close second.

The 1970s were a rough time for the Chicago Bears. They did not have a lot of success on the field. So management tried to make the games more fun for fans. Owner George Halas had the idea to hire cheerleaders. They were called the Honey Bears, and they became popular with fans. Halas promised the Bears would have cheerleaders on the sideline as long as he was alive.

Halas died in 1983. His daughter Virginia McCaskey took over the Bears. McCaskey disapproved of the

The Honey Bears were sideline fixtures at Chicago Bears games until the end of the 1985 season.

Chicago Bears players carry coach Mike Ditka off the field to celebrate their Super Bowl rout of the Patriots.

concept of cheerleading. She thought the role was disrespectful to women.

The Honey Bears were informed that 1985 would be their last year. They cheered for Chicago all the way through a storybook season. The Bears took a 15–1 record into the playoffs. Then they breezed through to the Super Bowl, where they beat the New England

Patriots 46–10. That day—January 26, 1986—was the last time the Bears had cheerleaders on the field.

And the Bears have not been champions since. They have had some great teams, but nothing close to the 1985 squad. They returned to the Super Bowl after the 2006 season but lost. They have only reached the NFC championship game two other times since the Honey Bears were disbanded.

THE CURSE GETS WORSE

Meanwhile, the Curse of the Billy Goat lingered in Chicago. In 2003 the Cubs were five outs away from a trip to the World Series. A Florida Marlins batter hit a foul fly ball. Cubs left fielder Moises Alou thought he could catch it. But a fan reaching for the ball knocked it away. The Marlins rallied for eight runs in that inning. They won the next game too, ending the Cubs' season.

HEISMAN HEX
PEAKING TOO EARLY

The Heisman Trophy is awarded to the nation's top college football player each season. It should be a sign of even better things to come. But for many Heisman winners, the award has been their career peak. Everything was downhill from that point forward.

Star athletes face incredible pressure to succeed. Sometimes they fail to meet expectations—their own, or those of the fans and media. Certain players have skills better suited to college football than to the NFL game.

Whatever the cause, there's a pattern of Heisman winners fizzling and fading in the pros. It seems to be

Unfortunately for Tim Tebow, winning the Heisman Trophy did not lead to great success in the NFL.

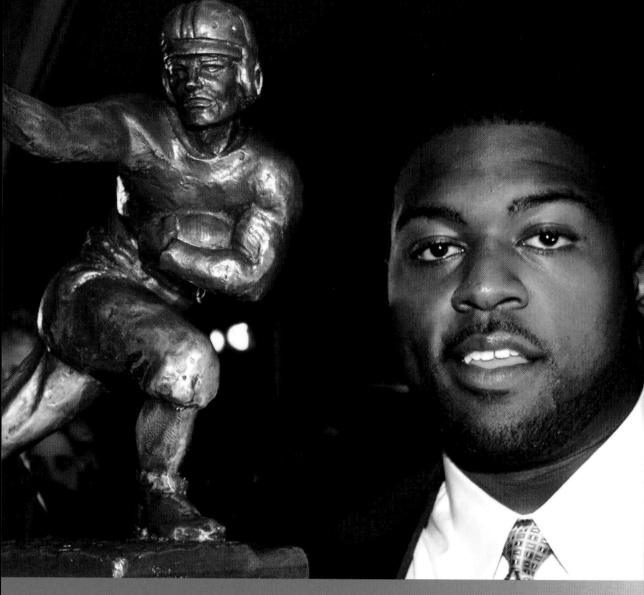

Wisconsin running back Ron Dayne won the Heisman Trophy in 1999. But he was a bust in the NFL.

especially difficult for quarterbacks. Many of them have gone on to become flops in the NFL. Florida's Tim Tebow is just one recent example. He did help guide the Denver Broncos to the playoffs in 2011. But he only started 18 NFL games in his brief career.

Meanwhile, consider this list: Aaron Rodgers, John Elway, Tom Brady, Joe Montana, Peyton Manning, Dan Marino. The best modern NFL quarterbacks were good college players. None of them won the Heisman Trophy.

BEFORE THE BIG GAME

The Heisman Hex does not just apply to the winners' NFL careers. Heisman hype can be disruptive if the winner is practicing for the national championship game. Over a 15-year span starting in 2000, the Heisman winner played for the title 11 times. They won four. Tebow won the Heisman in 2007. His Florida Gators won the national title in 2006 and 2008.

CURVE CURSE
ILLEGAL STICK TRIPS KINGS

The Los Angeles Kings were playing the Montreal Canadiens in the 1993 Stanley Cup Final. Los Angeles was looking for its first National Hockey League (NHL) championship. The Canadiens had won more titles than any other team. They added another Stanley Cup to their trophy case when the series turned in an unusual way.

After winning Game 1 in Montreal, the Kings led 2–1 with less than two minutes left in Game 2. Then Canadiens coach Jacques Demers asked the referees to check Kings defenseman Marty McSorley's stick. It was curved more than the NHL rule allowed. McSorley was given a penalty. The Canadiens scored on the power play to tie the game. Then they won in overtime.

The Kings finally broke through and won their first Stanley Cup in 2012.

The Kings were stunned, and the Canadiens took advantage. Montreal won the last three games to win their twenty-fourth Stanley Cup. The Kings did not get back to the finals for 19 years. But they did win their first Stanley Cup in 2012.

But is it possible the curse was actually on the Canadiens? According to McSorley and the Kings, the Canadiens knew exactly whose sticks should be checked. They believed the Canadiens spied on their equipment room. Since the stick flap, Montreal has not even reached the Stanley Cup Finals. Before then, the Canadiens' longest gap between Stanley Cups had been 13 years.

11

JAPANESE JINX
THE COLONEL'S REVENGE

Most professional baseball teams in Japan have a US player or two on the roster. Sometimes those players are winding down their careers. Occasionally a player will land back in the major leagues after his time in Japan. Then there are Americans who become Japanese legends, such as Randy Bass.

Bass hit only nine home runs in 130 major league games. But his power was unleashed with the Hanshin Tigers. The team plays in Osaka, the second-largest city in Japan. Over a five-year span, Bass hit 200 home runs for the Tigers. That is more than one every three games.

Randy Bass celebrates the Hanshin Tigers' victory in the 1985 Japan Series.

In 1985 Bass hit 54 homers and led the Tigers to their only Japan Series title. The celebration in downtown Osaka was wild. Fans shouted the name of each player on the team. Then a person in the crowd resembling that player jumped into the Dotonbori River. But nobody in the crowd looked like Bass, the brawny, bearded American. Instead the group snagged a statue of Colonel Sanders from a nearby Kentucky Fried Chicken restaurant. Then the fans tossed that into the water. Like Bass, the Colonel was American and had a beard.

As the years passed, the Tigers struggled to match the success of their 1985 season. Talk of a curse grew until a construction crew found the statue in 2009. Was the hex broken? Five years later, the Tigers were runners-up—a step in the right direction, at least.

Workers pose with the statue of Colonel Sanders after fishing it out of the Dotonbori River in 2009.

12

MASTERS MYTH
THE PAR 3 CONTEST JINX

The Masters golf tournament has many traditions. The winner gets a green jacket every year. Fans enjoy seeing the blooming azaleas and walking the hilly course. Another custom is the nine-hole Par 3 Contest, the day before the first round begins. Participants play nine holes on a smaller, nearby course. It is a casual, friendly game. Players invite friends and family. Many of the participants' children walk the course wearing the same white jumpsuits that the caddies wear. Players often swing from their opposite side. Spectators take selfies with the stars.

Phil Mickelson and his daughter, Amanda, enjoy the 2005 Masters Par 3 Contest.

Tiger Woods, *right*, receives congratulations from Mark O'Meara and Arnold Palmer after a hole-in-one at the 2004 Masters Par 3 Contest.

The day is all for fun and fun for all. Well, except for the unlucky winner. Not once since the Par 3 Contest began in 1960 has the winner also won the Masters the same year. Tiger Woods once acknowledged he purposely hit into the water on the last hole of the Par 3 Contest to make sure he did not win it. In the 2004 Par 3 Contest, Woods tied with Padraig Harrington and Eduardo Romero. He skipped the playoff. Masters officials cited a "prior engagement." Harrington beat Romero in the tiebreaker.

"I'm Irish," Harrington said. "There can't be a jinx for me."

Phil Mickelson won the Masters that year. Harrington tied for thirteenth.

FATHER KNOWS BEST

Ben Crenshaw won the Masters in 1984 and 1995. He won the Par 3 Contest in 1987. Crenshaw's father warned him of the curse that year when he took the lead to the last tee box. "Hit it in the water," his dad said. Crenshaw ignored the advice. He hit it straight and won the contest. When the weekend was over, Larry Mize was the Masters champion. Crenshaw tied for fourth.

HONORABLE MENTIONS

The Curse of the Black Sox—Eight Chicago White Sox players were found guilty of taking money from gamblers to lose the 1919 World Series on purpose. The White Sox did not win the title again until 2005.

Portland Trail Blazers Centers Curse—Bill Walton, Sam Bowie, and Greg Oden were all centers drafted by the Blazers with one of the top two picks. All three developed nagging injuries that shortened their careers.

The Cleveland Curse—The Cleveland Browns were NFL champions in 1964, two seasons before the Super Bowl was first staged. No major Cleveland team has won a championship since. The Browns, the Cleveland Indians, and the Cleveland Cavaliers proceeded to put their fans through decades of frustration, with late-game collapses and disappointing finishes galore.

The Curse of Billy Penn—The Philadelphia 76ers were National Basketball Association (NBA) champions in 1983. Then Philadelphia teams had a hard time winning titles. Some people pointed to construction of a skyscraper in 1987 that became the tallest building in the city. Previously the statue of state founder William Penn was the highest point in Philadelphia. When a new skyscraper was built in 2007, workers put a figurine of William Penn on top. The Phillies won the World Series the next year.

Curse of the Minnesota Twins Trees—The Twins opened Target Field in 2010 with 14 spruce trees planted behind center field. Hitters complained the trees were a distraction as they tried to watch pitches coming from the mound. The team removed the trees the next year. After winning their sixth division title in nine years in 2010, the Twins lost an average of 96 games over the next four seasons.

GLOSSARY

custom
A tradition in a culture or society.

generation
People born around the same time.

interception
A pass in a football game that is caught by a player on the defense.

Japan Series
The championship series of Japanese professional baseball, played between the winners of the Central League and the Pacific League.

perspective
A way of looking at a situation; viewpoint.

preseason game
A game that does not count in the standings.

rally
A sustained stretch of success that helps a player or team catch up to their opponents.

spectacle
A remarkable and dramatic sight.

FOR MORE INFORMATION

Books

Berman, Len. *The Greatest Moments in Sports: Upsets and Underdogs.* Naperville, IL: Sourcebooks, 2012.

Ferris, Julie Alfriend. *Badges, Egg Salad, and Green Jackets: The Masters A to Z.* Herndon, VA: Mascot Books, 2012.

Tibbals, Geoff. *Ripley's Sports: Believe It or Not!* Orlando, FL: Ripley Publishing, 2010.

Websites

To learn more about the Legendary World of Sports, visit **booklinks.abdopublishing.com**. These links are routinely monitored and updated to provide the most current information available.

INDEX

ABOUT THE AUTHOR

Dave Campbell has been a sportswriter for the Associated Press since 2000. He graduated from the University of St. Thomas in St. Paul, Minnesota, with a degree in print journalism, and he lives in Minneapolis with his wife and son. He was born in Illinois and raised in Wisconsin, developing a passion for sports and an interest in writing as a youth. He does not believe in curses, but he loves to tell (and hear) a good story.